Hunterdon County
A Millennial Portrait

Photography

Walter Choroszewski

Introduction

Governor Christine Todd Whitman

Published in cooperation with

Hunterdon Museum of Art

Published by

Aesthetic Press, Inc.
Somerville, New Jersey

Dedicated to the people of Hunterdon County.

Hunterdon County, A Millennial Portrait
© 1999 Aesthetic Press, Inc., All Rights Reserved.
All photographs © 1999 Walter Choroszewski,
All Rights Reserved.

Edited and designed by Walter Choroszewski.
Printed in China - First Printing 1999.

ISBN 0-933605-08-0

Walter Choroszewski

As a photographer, author and lecturer, Walter Choroszewski has been presenting the best of New Jersey since 1980, and has published numerous books and calendars on the state. Walter, his wife, Susan, son, Joe, and their English Springer Spaniel, "Beans," live in the village of South Branch.

Aesthetic Press, Inc.
Box 5306, Somerville, NJ 08876-1303   Tel: 908 369-3777

Opposite - Aerial view of Clinton.

Overleaf - Delaware River sunrise, Milford.

Hunterdon

People have compared Hunterdon County to a storybook land with its general stores, vintage churches and tranquil villages. Hunterdon County does seem like someplace that you might find illustrated in the pages of an old fairy tale.

That's Hunterdon County at the dawn of the new millennium, and I'm lucky enough to call it home.

I was raised on my parents' farm, Pontefract, in the countrified hamlet of Oldwick. After spending so much of our early married years living in neighboring Somerset County, my husband, John, and I moved our own family back to Pontefract where we live today.

Everyone knows that I'm a big fan of the whole state of New Jersey, but there's something special about Hunterdon…

Hunterdon County's history is as fertile as its soil. Established in 1714, the county was named for the popular New Jersey Governor Robert Hunter. Some fifty years later, it would provide vital passage for Revolutionary War troops. General George Washington, himself, resided in the county for a time, in Lambertville's Richard Holcombe House.

Hunterdon County boasts deep agricultural roots as well. In the 1800s, apple and peach crops spawned a flourishing produce industry there. Later, the county became a prosperous dairy farming center. Although many of the farm fields have sprouted a new crop—"houses," cattle still graze the rural fields, and pick-your-own farms and roadside stands still offer Hunterdon's finest "Jersey Fresh" produce.

Today, retail and restaurants, more than agriculture, bolster Hunterdon's economic base. Yet despite its tremendous growth, the county has succeeded in preserving its bucolic character. Maybe what makes Hunterdon County so special is that it's a place where you can go back in time and imagine our state as it was when our parents were young, and even before.

When I think about Hunterdon County, I think of storied Clinton, the quintessential small town, with its quaint shops, its homespun hospitality, and its famous mills. I think of Victorian Lambertville; of picturesque Frenchtown on the east bank of the Delaware River; of the covered bridge crossing the Wickecheoke Creek between Sergeantsville and Rosemont— the last of its kind in the state. I think of charming Flemington, home of the agricultural fair and the historic courthouse; of the silos that speckle the landscape in Raritan and Readington Townships; of the Vollendam Windmill in Holland Township; of the little villages of Mount Pleasant, Little York and Everittstown; of the Round Valley and Spruce Run reservoirs.

I also think of Hunterdon County as a haven for recreation and relaxation. There are, for example, the colorful gardens and groves of the Hunterdon Arboretum— originally a nursery, now a botanical gem and home of the county park system. Hunterdon's parklands feature nature trails, rocky cliffs, fields and streams on over 4,700 acres. Beyond the scenic beauty of these parks, Hunterdon's roadside landscapes offer picture-postcard vistas around every corner.

Each July, hot air balloons fill the skies at the New Jersey Festival of Ballooning in Readington and like the returning shad, each spring thousands of people return to Lambertville to enjoy the festivities of Shad Fest. Festivals and fairs, pancake breakfasts and church dinners, parades and concerts in the park... all are commonplace in the life of Hunterdon County.

Some people say that Hunterdon County is still New Jersey's best kept secret. I think it's a secret worth telling.

Craig Shelton, the chef at the Ryland Inn in Whitehouse Station, is telling it with his exquisite cuisine. Bruce Williams Zaccagnino is telling it with his popular Northlandz miniature wonderland. Homespun artisans are telling it with their pottery, pictures and glass— artisans such as Toshiko Takaezu, internationally known potter, Walter Chandoha, garden photographer extraordinaire, and Don Gonzales, a modern-day glass blower.

Photographer Walter Choroszewski, whose profession is showcasing New Jersey on film, has now captured Hunterdon County's unique essence with this extraordinary compilation of photographs— both landscape and portrait. Over the years, Choroszewski has developed a special fondness for Hunterdon. He recently completed a book of photographs on Lambertville and has published many a Hunterdon County image in the promotion of New Jersey.

What a wonderful collaboration between Hunterdon Museum of Art and Walter Choroszewski— presenting this photographic portrayal of Hunterdon County and celebrating the county's scenic beauty and unique character.

***Hunterdon County, A Millennial Portrait** is a special window to the county— a view that shows what makes Hunterdon such a priceless part of New Jersey's culture. Take in the enchanting images that await you. Learn the secret of Hunterdon County. Then pass it along.*

Christine Todd Whitman
Governor
State of New Jersey

The Oldwick General Store, Tewksbury.

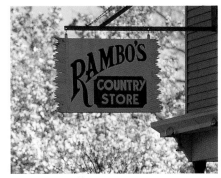

Above - General store display,

Hunterdon Historical Museum, Clinton.

Right - Rambo's Country Store, Califon.

Far Right - Peacock's Country Store, Wertsville.

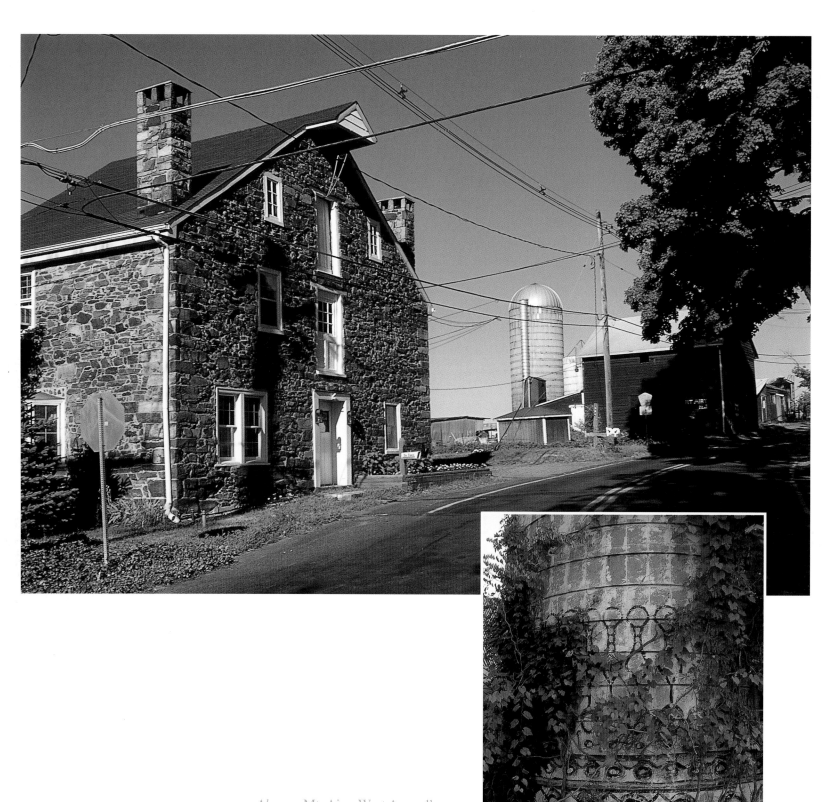

Above - Mt. Airy, West Amwell.

Right - Artistic silo, Bethlehem Township.

Hunterdon Museum of Art, 1836 stone mill, Clinton.

Above - Ken Lockwood Gorge, South Branch
Raritan River, Lebanon Township.
Left - Musconetcong River, Bloomsbury.

Sunrise,

Neshanic River,

East Amwell.

Above - Twin bridges, High Bridge.

Right - The Great Crate Race, Sergeantsville.

Opposite - Aerial of the Flemington

Circle, Routes 202 and 31.

Above - G.A.R. Monument,

1900, West Amwell.

Top & Left - VFW

Post 5119, Glen Gardner.

Opposite Right - American Legion

Post 113, Frenchtown.

Opposite Top - American Legion

Post 120, Lambertville.

Above - Old Red Mill,

Hunterdon Historical Museum, Clinton.

Right - Farm, Kingwood Township.

Flemington Free Public Library, Flemington.

Above - Readington Library, Whitehouse Station.

Left - Oldwick Library, Tewksbury.

Above - Statue of

"Little Chamomile Man,"

Merck's courtyard.

Left - Walking through Merck's

five-acre wooded courtyard

at its world headquarters,

Whitehouse Station.

The atrium of
Merck & Co., Inc.'s
world headquarters,
Whitehouse Station.

Above - Black River &
Western steam engine,
Raritan Township.
Top Right - Train mural, Stockton.
Right - West Portal Historic
Society, former municipal
building, Bethlehem Township.

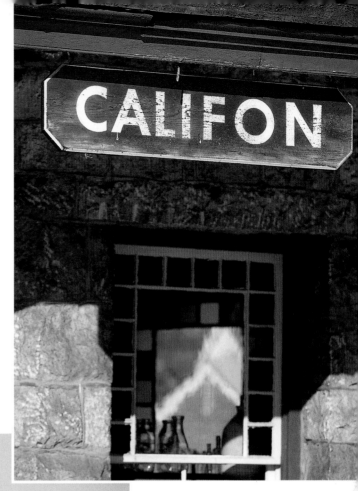

Above - Califon
Railroad Station.
Left - Ringoes
Railroad Station.

Hyman Salzberg, Egg Merchant, Kingwood.

Bruce Williams Zaccagnino, Northlandz creator, Flemington.

Dr. Frank DeCavalcante, Educator, Hunterdon Central H.S.

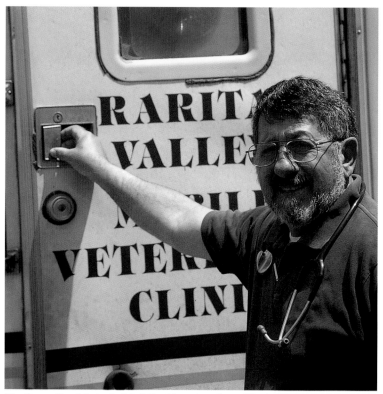

Dr. Sam Occhipinti, Mobile Veterinarian, Three Bridges.

Right - Don Gonzales,

Glass Artist, Delaware Township.

Opposite - Familiar Faces.

Above & Left - Whistle Stop

Farm & Nursery, Ringoes.

Above - Homestead
Farm Market,
Lambertville.
Right - Open House,
Readington River
Buffalo Farm,
Readington.

Above - Grandin.

Top - Lambertville.

Right - Moonset, East Amwell.

Spruce Run State Park,

Union Township.

Liberty Village, Flemington.

Above - Flea market,
West Amwell.
Left - Annual
town-wide flea
market, Hampton.

Raritan Township

Clinton Township

Delaware Township

Flemington

Clinton

Flemington

Union Township

Hampton

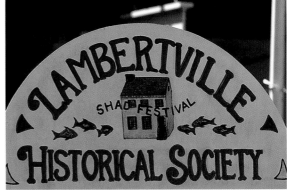

Lambertville

Oldwick

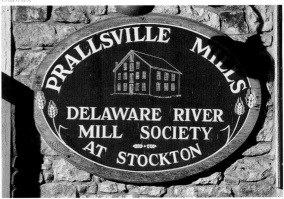

Stockton

Right - Sign, Hunterdon Museum

of Art, Clinton.

Opposite - Signs of Hunterdon County.

Above - Flemington and Raritan Township.

Top - Milford.

Right - Tewksbury Township.

County map on Hunterdon County

Administration Building, Flemington.

Right - Microwave tower, Cherryville.

Overleaf - Hoffmans Crossing.

Above - Farm pond, Tewksbury.

Opposite - Canoeing, Raritan River, Clinton.

Hillside view, High Bridge.

Church steeples, Lambertville.

Hereford cattle:

Right - Tewksbury.

Opposite - East Amwell.

Bikes near towpath, Frenchtown.

Bike at the Locktown Grange.

Above - Welcome sign, Clinton.

Left & Opposite - Annual river clean-up by volunteers of the South Branch Watershed Association, Raritan River, Clinton.

Overleaf - Farmscape, Holland Township.

Whitetail deer:

Above - Tewksbury Township.

Left - Lebanon Township.

56

Above & Right - Deer Path County Park,

Readington Township.

Sunlit porch, Milford.

Swing shadows, Bloomsbury.

Right - A young
bike rider in Milford.
Opposite - Dogwood,
Holland Township.

Union Hotel,

Flemington.

Reenactment of Lindbergh Trial,

Hunterdon County Court House, Flemington.

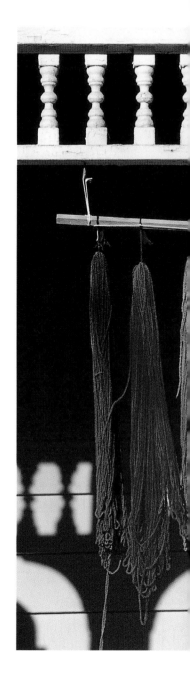

Quilting,

Prallsville Mills,

Stockton.

Above - Colored yarn, store display, Clinton.

Right - Sheep farm, Tewksbury.

Above - Autumn display at The Frenchtown Inn, Frenchtown.

Top - Farm Market, Fairmount, Tewsksbury.

Right - Hot air balloons, Readington.

Flemington Agricultural Fair,

Raritan Township.

Above - Ashton Farm,
Lebanon Township.
Left - Horse farm,
Clinton Township.

Above - Horse farm,

Tewksbury Township.

Left - Blue ribbon winner,

Flemington Agricultural Fair,

Raritan Township.

David Reynolds Tavern, 1783, Union Township.

Spring, Delaware Township.

Chef Craig Shelton,

The Ryland Inn,

Whitehouse.

Church dinner,

Lebanon United Methodist Church,

Lebanon Borough.

Lone tree,

East Amwell.

Vollendam Windmill,

Holland Township.

Flemington Speedway, Raritan Township.

Above - The Harmonizers, Borough Park, Flemington.

Opposite - The Hunterdon Symphony, Deer Path Park, Readington.

Autumn leaves:

Opposite - Bethlehem.

Right - Kingwood.

Califon Historical Museum, Califon.

Laundry day, Baptistown.

Toshiko Takaezu,

Artist,

Franklin.

Walter Chandoha,

Photographer,

Franklin.

Left - Round
Valley State Park,
Clinton Township.
Opposite - Teetertown Ravine
Nature Preserve,
Lebanon Township.

Above - View from Cokesbury Road, Clinton Township.

Left - Face painting, Flemington Fair, Raritan Township.

Frenchtown.

Bikers, Ken Lockwood Gorge,

Lebanon Township.

Green Sergeant's Covered Bridge, Delaware Township.

Above - Spring blossoms, Stanton.

Left - Red barns, Delaware Township.

Top - Sand Brook, Delaware Township.

Horse portrait, Alexandria.

Historic fountain, Flemington.

Walking along the towpath,

Delaware & Raritan Canal,

Prallsville Mills, Stockton.

Above - Califon.

Right - Millstone,

Hunterdon Historical

Museum, Clinton.

Above - Front porch scarecrows, Oldwick.

Opposite - Franklin Elementary School, Quakertown.

Overleaf - Delaware River, Frenchtown.

Left - Dvoor Farm, Raritan Township.

Top Left - Farmscape, Raritan Township.

Farmscape, Delaware Township.

Above - Spring, Alexandria.

Right - Aerial, Stockton.

Opposite - Aerial, Readington.

Above - Cliffs along the Delaware River, Raven Rock.

Right - Miniature wonderland, Northlandz, Flemington.

New Jersey Festival of Ballooning,

Solberg Airport, Readington.

Above - 4th of July decorations, Lebanon Borough.

Right - Miss Allonia, Memorial Day, Lambertville.

Above - Flag Day Bicycle Parade, Clinton.

Overleaf - Sunrise, Raritan Township.

General Store, Sergeantsville.

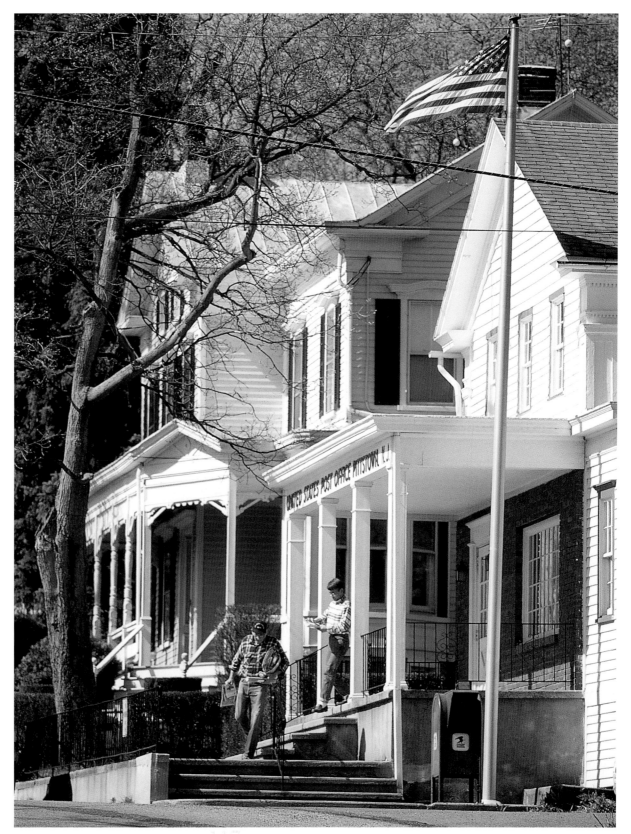

Former Post Office, Pittstown.

Left - Three Bridges

Reformed Church, Readington.

Opposite - Hunterdon Arboretum,

Clinton Township.

Overleaf - Winter, Raritan

River, Ken Lockwood Gorge,

Lebanon Township.

HUNTERDON MUSEUM OF ART

Hunterdon County, A Millennial Portrait represents a partnership among business, the arts and the community. Each advance sale helped make it possible to publish this book and at the same time supported the Hunterdon Museum of Art. It was a collaborative effort which successfully recognized Walter Choroszewski's photographic and publishing talents and the Museum's financial needs and strong community support.

The Museum is proud to be part of this collaboration. Like the county, Hunterdon Museum of Art is a mix of old and new. Housed in an 1836 stone mill on the bank of the South Branch of the Raritan River, the Museum exhibits traditional and contemporary art by both regional and internationally recognized artists. Many who wander into this historic building are surprised when they discover nontraditional work, but then Hunterdon County holds many surprises. Walter Choroszewski's beautiful photographs of the people and places of Hunterdon will be a lovely introduction for those who do not know the county and a congenial reminiscence for those who live here.

The Patron, Sponsors, Contributors and Friends listed below responded enthusiastically to this project. We are grateful for their support.

Marjorie Frankel Nathanson
Executive Director
Hunterdon Museum of Art

Cindi Hewitt
Co-chair
The Millennial Portrait Project

Dr. Beate Stych
Co-chair
The Millennial Portrait Project

PATRON

Merck & Co., Inc.

Whitehouse Station

Merck & Co., Inc. is a global research-driven pharmaceutical company that discovers, develops, manufactures and markets a broad range of human and animal health products, directly and through its joint ventures, and provides pharmaceutical benefit services through Merck-Medco Managed Care. Merck is headquartered in Whitehouse Station, Hunterdon County, NJ.

SPONSORS

Clinton Book Shop
Clinton

The Mathews Team at RE/MAX of Flemington
Flemington

Sprint
Clinton

CONTRIBUTORS

Barbara and Philippe Baumann
Hampton

Bob Beatty
Clinton

Cathy Cademartori
Clinton

Califon Historical Society
Califon

Jacqueline Cerenzo, CRS, GRI
Flemington

Clinton Canoe Company
Clinton

Cortes & Hay, Inc.
Flemington

Mary Dempsey & Pat Williams
Clinton

George M. Dilts, Attorney-at-Law
Flemington

Economic Concepts, Inc.
Annandale

Flemington Car and Truck Company
Flemington

The General Store of Oldwick
Oldwick

Huggables Hallmark
Whitehouse Station

Hunterdon County Democrat Newspapers
Flemington

Township of Kingwood
Baptistown

Market Roost Fine Catering & Restaurant
Flemington

Walter John O'Brien
Whitehouse Station

Lee B. Roth Law Offices
Flemington

The Ryland Inn
Whitehouse

Stone Mill Shop
Clinton

Dr. Beate Stych
Glen Gardner

Summit Bank
Hunterdon County locations

Time to Read Books
Flemington

Weichert Realtors
Clinton

FRIENDS

Louise & Thomas Agin
Rocky Alberty
Mr. and Mrs. Terry Allworthy
Carol and Michael J. Amato
Beverly M. Attinson
Helen Axel
Bearpaw Leather Shop
Christine Bennedsen
Daniel Bernstein
Nancy Bittner
Black River & Western Railroad
Borough of Bloomsbury, Mayor & Council
Dr. and Mrs. Paul A. Bogden
Bohren and Bohren Engineering
Julia Brown
Tom and Eva Burrell
Bush Excavating
Dr. and Mrs. Robert Caccavale
Larry & Barbara Carlbon
Mr. and Mrs. Russell H. Carlson
Pat Catanzareti Family
Clinton Car and Truck, Mark Porcaro
Clinton Township, Board of Adjustment
Clinton Township, Employees
Clinton Township, Planning Board
Coldwell Banker, Readington Office
Carol C. Comerford
Commerce Bank
Cindy and Bob Czaskos
Judy Davis
Pamela Deckman
Rosanne DeTorres & Lorraine Spanier
Eleanor Connell School of Dance
David J. Ennis & Associates
Dr. and Mrs. Eugene P. Fazzini
Jamie and Robert Fenlon
Janet Finley and Mike Forney
Flemington Fur Co.
Mr. and Mrs. Lewis Fletcher

Mr. and Mrs. Harry Fuerstenberger
Gebhardt & Kiefer, P.C.
Gebhardt Family (Virginia G. Dearborn)
Jim and Marjorie Goff
Barbara Granfield
Leni and Herb Grossman
Sandy and Lou Grotta
Elizabeth and Alexander Guest
Melissa and Gene Haplea
Virginia Harder and Ralph Harder
Gene and Betty Jean Hartsell
Cindi Hewitt
Lidia and Frank Hickman
Brian C. Hill
Bill Hindle
Jim Hindle
John Hindle, Jr.
Tripp Hindle
Kimberlee Hoey
Hunterdon Museum of Art, Staff
Maureen Huntington
Meg and Howard Jacobs
Margaret Kennard Johnson
Lora W. Jones
Maralon and James Jones
Mr. and Mrs. Morry Kapitan
June and Ira Kapp
Linda Young Kennedy
Krause's Flowers & Gifts
Jan and Bill Kreutel
The Laitem Family
Liberty Village Premium Outlets
Teresa Maher
Alexandra Alley Manning
Tony Martino
Mark Mazzatta
Mr. and Mrs. H. Clay McEldowney
Pamela Anne McGowan
John and Pamela McGuire

Catherine and Gary McVicker
Kathy Menzel
Blanche Milheim
Patricia A. Millar
Muller Toyota, Inc.
Marjorie F. Nathanson
The Nelson Family
Dr. and Mrs. S. Occhipinti
Frank Painter and Ingrid Renard
Raritan Valley Community College
Township of Readington
V. Eugene Refalvy
Dr. Yale and Mrs. Ilene Richmond
Ms. Berda S. Rittenhouse
Anne, Jain and Ken Rosenthal
George J. Sabol, D.D.S.
Mr. and Mrs. Alexander N. Salem
Mr. and Mrs. Stanley Sawczuk
Gloria and Harlan Schackner
Elizabeth B. Schley
Frank Rainer Schmidt, Architect
Mr. and Mrs. Rick Secrest
Patricia Segreaves
The Sena Family
Dr. Joseph Shannon
Shop on Main Street/CEA
Pam Shjarback
Elizabeth & George Shufflebotham
Ellen Siegel and Robert B. Haines
Mr. and Mrs. Adam Siodlowski
Carol Smigelsky
Wendy Sternberg
Barbro "Barbie" Terner
Ed and Clarie Turkiewicz
The Twanmoh - Charney Family
David E.W. and Julianne S. Vaughan
Diane Wigbers
Grace L. Wise
William Wright and Maria Wright

Green Sergeant's Covered Bridge, Delaware Township.